OWLS

Owl Magic for Kids

To Matthew, Maria, Emily, Tom, and Camille, with special thanks to
Doris, Barb, and Leanne.   *— Neal Niemuth*

**For a free catalog describing Gareth Stevens Publishing's list of high-quality books
and multimedia programs, call 1-800-542-2595 (USA) or 1-800-461-9120 (Canada).
Gareth Stevens Publishing's Fax: 414-225-0377.
See our catalog, too, on the World Wide Web: http://gsinc.com**

Library of Congress Cataloging-in-Publication Data

Niemuth, Neal D., 1960-
    Owl magic for kids / by Neal D. Niemuth; illustrations by
John F. McGee.
        p. cm. — (Animal magic for kids)
    Based on Owls for kids. 1995.
    Includes index.
    Summary: Information about the physical characteristics, habits,
and natural environment of snowy owls is woven into a story.
    ISBN 0-8368-1632-3 (lib. bdg.)
    1. Owls—Juvenile literature. 2. Snowy owl—Juvenile literature.
[1. Owls. 2. Snowy owl.] I. McGee, John F., ill. II. Title. III. Series.
QL696.S8N536   1996
598.9'7—dc20   96-15301

First published in this edition in
North America in 1996 by
Gareth Stevens Publishing
1555 North RiverCenter Drive, Suite 201
Milwaukee, Wisconsin 53212 USA

Based on the book, *Owls for Kids*, text © 1995 by Neal D. Niemuth, with illustrations by
John F. McGee. First published in the United States in 1995 by NorthWord Press, Inc.,
Minocqua, Wisconsin. End matter © 1996 by Gareth Stevens, Inc.

Photographs © 1995: Dembinsky Photo Associates, Cover, 3, 10-11, 13, 20, 23, 28, 33,
36-37, 40, 41, 44, 45, Back Cover. John Hendrickson, 31, 34, 38, 46-47; Gerard Fuehrer,
14, 26, 39; Rod Planck, 4, 6.

Printed in the United States of America

1 2 3 4 5 6 7 8 9 99 98 97 96

by Neal Niemuth

OWLS

Owl Magic for Kids

Gareth Stevens Publishing
MILWAUKEE

I will never forget my winter vacation last year! When school let out, I ran home thinking about skiing and sledding all day long every day for two whole weeks. But I never did those things.

I found something a lot more interesting to keep me busy, something much more exciting. I found an owl near my house. My name is Jason and I'm 10 years old.

On my way home from school, I saw something sitting on top of a fence post at the edge of the field. It was white, and it had large, yellow eyes that stared at me as I walked by. At first I didn't know what it was. It just looked like a white blob with eyes. And I couldn't even see its legs or wings.

But then I could tell that it was a bird—the biggest bird I had ever seen.

Snowy owl

It was a snowy owl. I had seen pictures of them before and had always wanted to see one for real. This was my lucky day!

I ran to the house to tell my mom. I don't think she believed me at first. After all, no one had seen a snowy owl around here before.

"You're right, Jason," she said when she saw it too. "It's a snowy owl. You must have been looking very carefully to have spotted it against the snow."

As we watched, the owl glided near the ground and then flew back to its perch on top of the post. When it flew, its wings were wider than I could spread my arms—almost five feet, I guessed.

When my dad came home, the owl was gone. I was disappointed that he didn't get to see it too, but I figured it was probably hunting for dinner, and that we might see it again later.

Snowy owls usually live in the far north, where snow covers the ground much of the year and there aren't any trees. That's probably why it felt at home in our field—because it's a wide open space too.

The owl's white color provides camouflage, making it hard to spot in a snow-covered landscape. This helps the owl be less visible to the prey animals it eats. Owls especially like to eat mice, voles, and lemmings.

Snowy owl

    Snowy owls are more diurnal than most owls, meaning they are often active during the day. That's because in the tundra, where snowy owls live in summer, the sun almost never sets. So the owls are used to being active during the day.

The next day I told my friend Sarah about the owl in our field. She came over to my house because she wanted to see it too. She once did a report on owls in school, so she knows lots of neat stuff about them. She told me that during some winters, large numbers of snowy owls leave the Arctic and fly south, where people in Canada and the northern part of the United States can see them. The owls look for areas like their treeless homes, and are often found in open fields, along lake shores, and even at airports. That's why the owl was by our house—just like I guessed!

Snowy owls might fly south because the prey they eat have become scarce. Because most snowy owls have never seen a human, they are not afraid of people and will perch on church steeples and rooftops. That explained why the owl didn't fly when I walked by.

Sarah told me that female snowy owls have dark spots. Male snowy owls are almost pure white.

Snowy owl

We got to the edge of the field and I pointed to the post. The owl was back, sitting where I had first seen it. I got out my binoculars so we could see the owl better.

"Look what he's doing now," I told Sarah as I handed her the binoculars.

The owl had stretched its body out, and was bobbing its head up and down very quickly. As we watched, it sprang from its perch, flew part way across the field, and landed by a clump of grass sticking out of the snow. It looked around, then lowered its head to its feet. When it lifted its head again, we could see something small and dark in the owl's bill. It had caught a mouse! The owl then tilted its head back, and the mouse disappeared. I couldn't believe my eyes. The owl had swallowed the mouse whole.

Owls have excellent vision, both at night and during the day. They see much better than people can. Sarah said that the eyes of a snowy owl are almost as large as a person's, even though the owl only weighs about four pounds.

If human eyes grew as large for their body as an owl's, we'd have eyes as big as oranges!

Because its eyes are so big, an owl can't move them from side to side or up and down as we can. Instead, it has to turn its entire head if it wants to look in a different direction.

An owl can swivel its head from one side to the other so quickly it looks as if the owl is spinning its head all the way around.

Owls can't really spin their head in circles like some people think. But it sure looks like fun.

With their huge eyes, owls are able to spot far-off prey even at night. The head bobbing we had seen was the owl's way of getting a better guess of how far away the mouse was before flying to it.

Owls have built-in goggles to protect their eyes. In addition to a solid eyelid like we have, owls also have a see-through eyelid for each eye. When an owl is flying among branches or capturing prey, the clear eyelid closes so the eye is protected from injury. If you look closely as an owl blinks, you can sometimes see the extra eyelid glide across the eye.

Their wonderful vision and built-in goggles are a great help to owls. But there's one drawback. Because their eyes are so well designed for seeing in the dark, owls can't see color as well as people can. Scientists say that owl eyes are designed for gathering light instead of seeing color. So owls see a less colorful world than people see.

Snowy owl

I remembered that owls are also supposed to have excellent hearing. I looked closely at the owl as it sat on its perch. I didn't see any ears, so I wondered how it could hear so well.

Sarah told me that owls have small ear flaps on their heads, hidden below soft feathers. The disc-shaped feathers on an owl's face funnel noises into the ear opening.

These facial feathers act like a satellite dish for sound.

Some different kinds of owls, like the great horned owl, have tufts on their head that look like ears, but are really just feathers. They don't help the owl hear at all.

Instead, the tufts provide camouflage by breaking up an owl's outline. By changing the position of the tufts, owls also use them to indicate their moods.

What a great way to communicate!

Great horned owl

Owls also use their ears to find prey. As a matter of fact, some owls hear so well that they can catch prey without using their eyes. A barn owl might only hear the rustle of a mouse dashing across leaves on the ground. In a flash, it flies down and catches the mouse without seeing it. Other owls, like the great gray owl, perch in a tree and listen for mice running under the snow. They focus on the noise and dive feet-first into the snow to grab their prey. They don't see the mouse until they're ready to eat it!

With such wonderful vision and hearing, many owls don't even have to fly around to look for prey. Like the snowy owl in our field, they sit in one spot, looking and listening for prey before swooping down on it.

Their body structures make owls good predators. A single barn owl can catch as many as 11,000 mice during its lifetime. I think that shows that owls do an important job in nature.

Can you imagine how many mice there would be running around without owls? Some people even refer to owls as "mousetraps with wings."

Snowy owl

As we watched the owl during the middle of the day, it stopped looking around and just sat on top of the post. With binoculars, we could see that the owl often closed its eyes to sleep. I was amazed that the owl could stay warm in the winter cold. But I knew that the owl had good insulation, because one day I found one of the owl's feathers beneath its perch. The feather was soft and fuzzy—just like you'd find in a down coat. I could also see that the owl had downy feathers covering its feet to keep its toes warm.

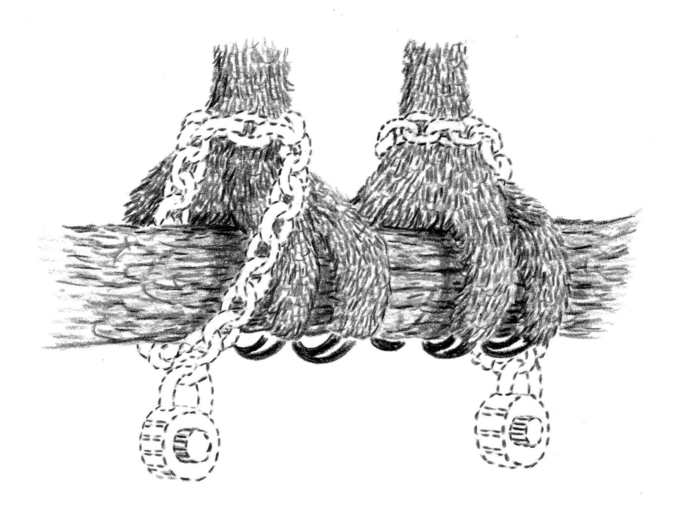

And when the owl was perched, its feet were tucked underneath its breast feathers, which also must help keep them warm.

But I knew that underneath those soft, downy feathers were curved, needle-sharp talons more than an inch long, which the owl used to catch and carry prey. When it slept, the owl's specially designed toes locked into position, preventing it from falling off its perch.

Owls eat their prey differently from many other animals. Like other birds, owls don't have teeth, so they can't chew their food. Instead, they eat it in chunks. Or if it is small enough, they eat the prey animal whole: bones, fur, teeth, and tail included!

A mouse or a rat usually goes down head first. Sometimes a young owl can't swallow the entire prey animal at once, and the young owl will sit in its nest with the prey animal's tail hanging out of its mouth, until the owl can swallow some more.

Owls aren't known for their good table manners.

Barn owl

After the owl had flown away to find dinner, Sarah and I walked over to the post to get a closer look at the perch. At the base of the post were several dark, fuzzy pellets. When we poked the pellets apart with a stick, we found the bones and skulls of animals the owl had eaten.

I figured that the owl was not able to digest all of the prey. So after eating the mouse, the owl coughed up a pellet, which contained parts of the mouse such as bones and fur. By looking at the pellets, we could tell what the owl had been eating!

The owl stayed by my house throughout the winter. But as the days got longer and warmer, I knew that the owl would soon leave for its home in the north. And that's exactly what happened. One day, when the sun was warm and the snow was beginning to melt, I looked for the owl in the usual place, but it wasn't there. Every evening after school, I looked for the owl, but it was nowhere to be seen.

Then one night, as the sun was going down and I was walking back to my house, I heard hooting coming from the woods down by the creek. I ran down the road toward the edge of the trees, and stopped to listen.

"Whoo, hoo hoo hoo hoo," came the voice of the owl. A moment later, I heard another owl join in, this time from the other side of the creek.

At first I hoped that it was my owl, even though I knew it probably had flown back to the Arctic tundra. It was getting late and almost too dark to see. But the next day was Saturday, so I planned to spend the day looking for the owl.

Right after breakfast, Dad and I left for the woods. I had the binoculars hanging around my neck, and both of us wore tall boots. We walked down the road and crossed the creek, and then we started hiking through the woods. Dad walked back and forth through the woods, as though he were looking for something.

Barn owl

Suddenly, Dad stopped. "Look up there, Jason," he whispered. "In that big oak tree."

I looked. At first, all I could see was a mass of branches and twigs, but then I saw the owl.

Two feather tufts poked up above the nest, and two enormous yellow eyes peered over the rim of the nest.

It was a great horned owl!

We could see that the owl was sitting on a nest. It was a female incubating her eggs—which meant that her mate was probably perched somewhere close by.

I studied the owl through the binoculars. She stared right back at me. Once in a while she blinked, but she didn't look like she was going to leave her nest. I was surprised that she had laid her eggs already. There was still snow on the ground, and the temperature was barely above freezing.

Great horned owl

Great horned owls

Dad told me that many species of owls lay their eggs in early spring. That way the babies have all summer to grow and learn how to hunt for themselves.

It would have been fun to watch her all day, but we knew we had better get going so we wouldn't disturb her.

Just before we got to some pines, the male owl flew from one of the trees. We had been standing quite close to him, but we heard no flapping or the "whoosh" of its wings going through the air above us.

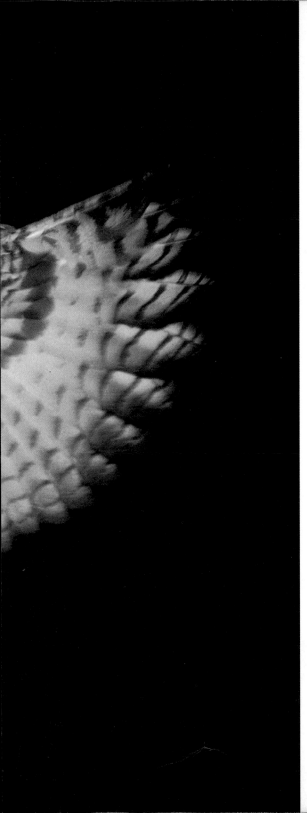

Dad explained that the shape and softness of owl feathers are different from those of many other birds.

In addition to keeping the bird warm, an owl's soft and downy feathers help it make less noise as it flies. The feathers on an owl's wings also have fine barbs to split wind currents flowing over the wing. That eliminates the whistling noise most bird wings make as they slice through the air.

It's easier for the owl to listen for prey when its wings aren't making any noise. It also prevents prey animals from hiding, because they can't hear the owl flying nearby.

Great horned owl

We walked over to the tree where the owl had been. As I expected, we found pellets underneath the tree, as well as a patch of smelly, black and white fur.

Yuck! The owl had eaten a skunk.

"They can't smell it," Dad said. "Even though owls can hear and see extremely well, they have a poorly developed sense of smell. The black and white stripes of a skunk warn most animals to stay away, but to a great horned owl, those stripes mean supper. Great horned owls are very adaptable. They'll even live in big cities, where they eat pigeons and rats."

Great horned owl

As we continued our walk, I thought some more about owl families. If a male owl doesn't already have a mate, he hoots at night to attract a female. Female owls are usually larger than males, but except for the size difference, it's hard to tell one from the other.

During courtship a male owl gives little gifts to a female. But an owl's idea of a nice present is a dead mouse. The two birds continue their courtship by grooming each other's feathers with their bills. After a few weeks, the female is ready to lay her eggs.

Saw-whet owl

Like other birds, owls incubate their eggs, keeping them warm in the nest until the eggs hatch. But unlike most other birds, owls don't build their own nests. Depending on the type of owl, it might use an old crow or hawk nest or lay its eggs in a woodpecker hole or hollow tree. Some owls, such as the snowy owl, even lay their eggs on the ground.

Owl eggs are rounder and less pointed than other birds' eggs. Great horned owls lay eggs about the size of the chicken eggs you may have in your refrigerator. Smaller owls, like the saw-whet owl, lay eggs the size of a big marble. The eggs of some small owls will hatch after 21 days of incubation, while the eggs of larger owls, such as the great horned owl, require up to 35 days of incubation. During this time, the female rarely strays from the nest and depends on the male to bring her food.

We didn't visit the nest again for several weeks because we didn't want to disturb the owls. But one Saturday morning, we headed for the woods. When we got close, I saw one of the adults fly from the nest. I looked at the nest with my binoculars. In it were two baby owls! They were covered with a thick gray fuzz that looked like sheep wool, and they were crouched down, holding very still. I started to move closer to the tree, then something surprised me.

Perched on a leaning tree only five feet above the ground was another baby owl. It must have fallen from the nest. As soon as I pointed it out to Dad, the young owl stood up straight, spread its wings, and began to sway back and forth. It glared at us, and then made a clicking noise by snapping its tongue against its bill.

"He's afraid," said Dad. "Right now he's trying to look big and fierce so he'll scare us away."

I wondered if we should try to put him back in the nest. Dad told me that the little owl was fine where it was. As a matter of fact, it probably left the nest on its own. Many young owls jump out of their nests before they can even fly. They climb onto a leaning tree, like the one in front of us, so predators can't get them.

There was no need to worry about the baby because the parents would return to take care of it. So we left.

Great gray owls

I didn't go back to the nest again, but several evenings I walked to the bridge to listen to the owl family. As it got dark, the parents would hoot back and forth to each other. The young owls screeched and hissed, begging for food. Even though I couldn't see them, I knew the babies were growing and that soon they would learn to live on their own.

Chances are good that you will see an owl one day. No matter where you live — in the forest, in the desert, in the country, or in town — owls are close by.

GLOSSARY

Arctic: Of or relating to the area surrounding the North Pole (page 13).

Camouflage: Markings or coloration that help an animal blend in with its surroundings (page 10).

Diurnal: Active during the day (page 12).

Prey: An animal that is hunted for food (page 14).

Species: A group of living things that have similar characteristics (page 34).

Talons: The claws of a bird, such as an owl, that are helpful in catching prey animals (page 27).

Tundra: The flat, treeless region of the Arctic that has permanently frozen subsoil (page 12).

ADULT-CHILD INTERACTION QUESTIONS

These are questions designed to encourage young readers to participate in further study and discussion of owls.

1. What is the biggest owl in North America? In the world?
2. One of an owl's ear flaps is slightly higher than the other. Why?
3. Do owls mate for life?
4. Are any species of owls endangered?
5. Baby owlets in a nest are sometimes very different in size. Why?
6. Why do owls migrate in winter?
7. Where would a great horned owl live in a city? A screech owl?

MORE BOOKS TO READ

All About Owls by Jim Arnosky (Scholastic)
The Owl in the Tree by Jennifer Coldrey (Gareth Stevens)
Owls by Markus Kappeler (Gareth Stevens)
Owls by George Michael (Child's World)
Owls by Herbert S. Zim (Morrow)
The World of Owls by David Saintsing (Gareth Stevens)

VIDEOS

The Great Gray Owl (Phoenix/BFA Films)
The Lady and the Owl (National Film Board of Canada)
Two Little Owls (Berlet Films)